Collective Biographies

TRAILBLAZING AMERICAN WOMEN
First in Their Fields

Barbara Kramer

Enslow Publishers, Inc.

40 Industrial Road   PO Box 38
Box 398   Aldershot
Berkeley Heights, NJ 07922   Hants GU12 6BP
USA   UK
http://www.enslow.com

Library of Congress Cataloging-in-Publication Data

Kramer, Barbara
    Trailblazing American women : first in their fields / Barbara Kramer.
        p.   cm. — (Collective biographies)
    Includes bibliographical references (p.) and index.
    Contents: Jane Addams—Madam C. J. Walker—Harriet Quimby—Jeannette
Rankin—Frances Perkins—Pearl S. Buck—Althea Gibson—Sandra Day
O'Connor—Marlene Sanders—Antonia C. Novello.
    ISBN 0-7660-1377-4
    1. Women—United States—Biography—Juvenile literature. 2. United States—
Biography—Juvenile literature. [1. Women Biography.] I. Title. II. Series.
CT3260.K73   2000
920.72'0973-dc21   99-41299
                                                                        CIP

Printed in the United States of America

10 9 8 7 6 5 4 3 2

To Our Readers: We have done our best to make sure all Internet addresses in this
book were active and appropriate when we went to press. However, the author and
the publisher have no control over and assume no liability for the material available
on those Internet sites or on other Web sites they may link to. Any comments or
suggestions can be sent by e-mail to comments@enslow.com or to the address on the
back cover.

Illustration Credits: AP/Wide World Photos, pp. 86, 93; Courtesy Ronald
Reagan Library, p. 83; Emma Edmunds White Collection, Lipscomb
Library, Randolph-Macon Woman's College, pp. 56, 63; Franklin D.
Roosevelt Library, p. 53; Jane Addams Memorial Collection, Special
Collections, University Library, University of Illinois at Chicago, pp. 8, 15;
Madam C.J. Walker Collection, Indiana Historical Society Library, #C2140,
p. 18; #C2225, p. 24; Montana Historical Society, Helena, pp. 36, 43;
National Air and Space Museum, Smithsonian Institution (SI Neg. No. A-
4133), p. 26; National Air and Space Museum, Smithsonian Institution (SI
Neg. No. 85-18319), p. 32; Photo courtesy of the International Tennis Hall
of Fame & Museum; Newport, RI, pp. 66, 73; Photograph by Dane
Penland, Collection of the Supreme Court of the United States, p. 76;
Program Support Center, Department of Health and Human Services, pp.
96, 102; U.S. Department of Labor, p. 46.

Cover Illustration: Program Support Center, Department of Health and
Human Services

Contents

Preface

What does it take to blaze a new trail, to do something that no one else has done? For the women in this book, it took a combination of talent and hard work. But most of all, it took courage. Often, being first meant facing criticism from those who did not accept their views or who did not believe that they were up to the job.

Sandra Day O'Connor was ranked third in her class when she graduated from law school in 1952, but she had trouble finding a job. Large law firms did not want to hire a woman lawyer. She would not be discouraged, and in 1981 she became the first woman to be sworn in as a U.S. Supreme Court justice.

When the United States entered World War I, Jane Addams spoke out for peace. Americans criticized her at the time, but fifteen years later she became the first American woman to win the Nobel Peace Prize. Jeannette Rankin, the first woman elected to the U.S. Congress, was also criticized for her efforts for peace in World War I.

Althea Gibson faced racial prejudice when she began a career in tennis. She was not allowed to play in tournaments held at all-white tennis clubs. Gibson broke the color barrier in tennis in 1950, and fourteen years later she did the same in golf.

The women in this book did not set out to be "first," but they were highly motivated to succeed. Their reasons to achieve were as varied as the careers they chose.

In 1911, Frances Perkins witnessed the deaths of 146 young women during a fire at the Triangle Shirtwaist Company in New York. She never forgot what she saw that day. She devoted her life to making sure that nothing like that would happen again. In 1933, she was appointed U.S. secretary of labor, the first woman to become a member of a president's cabinet.

Chronic illness as a child led Antonia C. Novello to become a doctor. Her dream was one day to help the children in her own neighborhood in Puerto Rico. She ended up helping children all across the United States when she became the first woman to be appointed to the position of U.S. surgeon general.

Pearl S. Buck hoped to use her writing to bring more understanding between two very different countries—the United States and China. In 1938, she became the first American woman to win the Nobel Prize in literature.

By achieving "firsts," these women have given boosts to other women, too. Madam C. J. Walker was the first African-American woman to become a self-made millionaire. She also made it possible for other African-American women to run their own businesses by training them to sell the hair care products she invented.

Marlene Sanders was the first woman to anchor a nighttime news show and the first woman vice president at a major television network. She used her position as vice president to encourage the network to hire women and minorities.

Harriet Quimby, a successful journalist, was looking for a story when she first discovered the excitement of flying. She became the first American woman to get a pilot's license, and, eight months later, she was the first woman to fly across the English Channel. Perhaps even more important was her vision of a future for women in flight. She predicted that one day women could make a living in aviation, carrying passengers and cargo or teaching others to fly.

Profiled here are ten of the many outstanding women who have forged their own career paths and made history. They represent a variety of professions and historical periods, and their unique stories show what it takes to blaze new trails. Each has opened doors for others to follow. And the triumphs continue: In July 1999, Colonel Eileen Marie Collins became the first woman to pilot a space shuttle. Still, we have yet to elect a woman president of the United States.

Even as the walls of gender and race come tumbling down, there are more barriers to cross, new doors to open. The courageous trailblazers on these pages have led the way for future pioneers.

Jane Addams

Jane Addams

Winner of the Nobel Peace Prize

When the United States entered World War I in 1917, Jane Addams was working for peace. Her actions angered many Americans, who said that it was un-American to oppose the war. They called Addams a traitor and a coward. Some of the harshest criticism came from the Daughters of the American Revolution (DAR), an organization that promotes patriotism and honors those who fought for America's independence. They revoked Addams's membership and called her the "most dangerous woman in America today."[1]

Almost fifteen years later, times and attitudes had changed. In 1931, Addams received the Nobel Peace Prize. The Nobel Prize is named after its founder,

Swedish scientist Alfred Nobel. Nobel awards are given in the areas of physics, chemistry, medicine, economics, literature, and peace. Addams was the first American woman to win the Nobel Peace Prize.

Jane Addams was born in Cedarville, Illinois, on September 6, 1860, about seven months before the start of the Civil War. Her father, John Addams, was a successful businessman and a friend of Abraham Lincoln. John Addams believed that slavery was wrong, but he did not fight in the Civil War. He was a pacifist, someone who does not believe in war or violence of any kind.

Jane was the youngest of five children. When Jane was only two years old, her mother died. Although her father remarried when Jane was eight, in those early years without a mother, Jane grew very attached to her father. He became an important influence in her young life. "I centered upon him all that careful imitation which a little girl ordinarily gives to her mother's ways and habits," she later wrote.[2]

Jane wanted to please her father, but she thought that she must be an embarrassment to him because of her physical condition. She had a slightly curved spine that caused her to walk with her head held to one side. Others may not have even noticed her awkwardness, but Jane was very aware of it. She saw herself as an "ugly, pigeon-toed little girl."[3]

Jane learned early on about the inequalities among people. She recalled one incident that occurred sometime before she turned seven. Her father had taken Jane with him on a business trip into town. They made a stop in the poor section of town, and for the first time Jane saw that not everyone lived as comfortably as she did. She asked her father "why people lived in such horrid little houses so close together."[4] After her father explained, Jane vowed that when she grew up, she would live in a big house but not in a wealthy part of town. Her house would be in a neighborhood like the one she saw that day.

After high school, Addams enrolled at Rockford Female Seminary in Rockford, Illinois, graduating in 1881. She then enrolled at Woman's Medical College of Pennsylvania in Philadelphia to study to become a doctor.

Poor health kept her from continuing her studies. Her spine was causing her a great deal of pain, and she underwent surgery to correct the problem. The surgery was successful, but she had a long recovery. Her health problems and her father's sudden death from a ruptured appendix left her feeling lonely and discouraged, with no real plan for her future. Using money left to her in her father's will, she began to travel.

In 1888, on a trip to Europe with her friend Ellen Gates Starr, Addams visited Toynbee Hall. The world's first settlement house, Toynbee Hall was located in one of London's worst slums. It was called a settlement house because volunteer workers lived, or settled, there among the people that they were trying to help. Now Addams knew what she wanted to do with her life. She and Starr decided that they would start their own settlement house. They returned to Illinois to put their plan into action.

Chicago, the second-largest city in the United States, was home to many European immigrants. These people came to America hoping for a better life but ended up living in crowded tenement houses. Those who found employment worked long hours in low-paying factory jobs. Many children were not able to go to school because they had to work to help their families.

Addams and Starr found a run-down mansion on Halsted Street, right in the center of Chicago's factory district. This became their settlement house, which opened in 1889. It was called Hull House, named after the home's builder, Charles J. Hull. "We had no definite idea what we were there to do," Addams later said. "But we hoped, by living among the people, to learn what was needed and to help out."[5]

They opened a day-care center in a cottage near Hull House. They started a kindergarten, a boys' club for older children, and vocational training for teenagers. Addams wanted the children in the community to have a place to play, so she and Starr had a playground built. They also added a gymnasium for recreation for all ages. Volunteers taught English to the immigrants and offered adult classes in art, music, and drama. Over time, the settlement grew to include thirteen buildings.

Hull House became a training center for young people interested in going into the field of social work. Volunteers came from all over the country to live and work there. Many of these volunteers went on to become leaders in social reform.

Addams continued to find new ways to help the community. She worked for legislation to improve working conditions in the factories and fought for child labor laws. These laws would prevent employers from hiring children younger than fourteen to work in the factories. Garbage, which piled up in the neighborhood streets, was a source of disease. In 1894, Addams applied to become district garbage inspector. Under her direction, garbage collection improved. In 1910, her first autobiography, *Twenty Years at Hull-House*, was published and quickly became a best-seller.

In 1914, with the outbreak of war in Europe, Addams turned her efforts to peace. In January 1915, she attended a convention of women in Washington, D.C. There she helped found the Woman's Peace Party, and she was named chairman of that organization.

That spring, she went to Europe to help organize an international women's peace movement. Through these organizations, she appealed to countries that were not fighting in the war and urged them to act as mediators for peace. At that time, the United States was one of those neutral countries. Americans did not want to get involved in the war. Then, after German submarines attacked American ships, Americans changed their minds about fighting. In 1917, the U.S. Congress voted to declare war on Germany.

Addams continued to speak out against the war. Her views now made Americans angry. They said that she should support the war effort. Even Addams's friends turned against her. Searching for another way to help the cause of peace during the war, Addams volunteered to work with the Department of Food Administration. That department, under the direction of Herbert Hoover, helped feed those who were starving in war-torn Europe.

When the war ended in 1918, Addams continued her efforts to get food to European countries. She expanded her work to include Germany. This made Americans even angrier with her. They did not think that she should be helping a country that had been their enemy.

In 1919, Addams traveled to Europe, where she helped found the Women's International League for Peace and Freedom (WIL). She was named president of the group. For the next few years, Addams spent much of her time traveling throughout Europe and Asia on behalf of the WIL. She gave speeches encouraging countries to work together. People in other parts of the world admired her work for peace. Gradually, people in the United States grew to respect her peace efforts as well.

Addams also continued her work at Hull House. In 1929, Hull House celebrated its fortieth birthday.

Jane Addams, right, holds a flag for peace. In 1931, Addams became the first American woman to win the Nobel Peace Prize.

The following year, Addams published her second autobiography, *The Second Twenty Years at Hull-House.*

Over the years, Addams was nominated to receive the Nobel Peace Prize several times. She was finally awarded the prize in 1931. Sadly, by that time, Addams was in poor health and was not able to make the trip to Sweden to receive the prize in person. Professor Halvdan Koht, a member of the Nobel Committee, spoke on her behalf. He recalled how she had worked for peace during World War I when others had criticized her efforts.

During her lifetime, Addams wrote eleven books and many articles about social problems and peace. She also served as president of the WIL from the time it was founded in 1919 until her death. She died on May 21, 1935, at the age of seventy-four. At the time of her death, New York Representative Caroline O'Day expressed the feelings of many when she said, "Miss Addams was one of the great women not only of our day but of all time. Her life was dedicated to the cause of humanity, her sympathies knew no boundaries of prejudice. She has become a symbol of tolerance and warm human understanding."[6]

Today, the original mansion that became Hull House is a museum on the campus of the University of Illinois at Chicago. Addams's work continues through the Hull House Association, which currently operates nearly one hundred programs for families in Chicago.

2

Madam C. J. Walker

Businesswoman and Self-Made Millionaire

At the 1913 National Negro Business League conference, Madam C. J. Walker rose to address the mostly male audience. "I started in business eight years ago with one dollar and fifty cents," she said. "[Now I am] giving employment to more than a thousand women."[1] Walker did not have money or a formal education. What she did have was good business instincts, a willingness to work hard, and a product that people needed. She developed a line of hair care products for black women, specially formulated for their hair texture. That venture made her the first African-American woman to become a millionaire.

Walker was born Sarah Breedlove on December 23, 1867, on a plantation near Delta, Louisiana. It

Madam C. J. Walker

was two years after the end of the Civil War, and Sarah, the third child of Owen and Minerva Breedlove, was the first in her family to be born free. After the Civil War, the Breedloves became share-croppers. That meant that they rented land from their former master, paying him a share, or portion, of their crops. It was often a large share, which kept the family poor in spite of all their hard work.

By the time Sarah was five years old, she was already working in the cotton fields with her family. On Saturdays, she helped her mother and her sister, Louvenia, with the laundry they took in to earn extra money. Sarah was only seven years old when both of her parents died, perhaps in a local epidemic of yellow fever, a deadly disease. For a while, the children tried to stay together on the farm. Unable to make a decent living as a sharecropper, Sarah's brother, Alex, moved west to Denver. Louvenia and Sarah stayed in Louisiana and supported themselves by taking in laundry.

In 1878, they moved to Vicksburg, Mississippi. Soon, Louvenia Breedlove married. Sarah lived with her sister and brother-in-law for a few years, but it was not a happy time. When Sarah was fourteen, she married too, partly to get away from her brother-in-law's cruelty.

Sarah's husband, Moses McWilliams, worked at odd jobs and Sarah continued to take in laundry. On June 6, 1885, their daughter, Lelia, was born. Two years later, Sarah's husband was killed. The facts of his death are not known today.

Sarah and her daughter then moved to St. Louis, Missouri. At that time, St. Louis was the third-largest city in the United States. People told Sarah that she could earn more money there from her laundry business. Sarah wanted Lelia to get an education and a chance at a better life. Because she had to work in the fields, Sarah had not been able to attend school when she was a child. She wanted life to be different for her daughter. For the next eighteen years, Sarah worked as a laundrywoman, saving up enough money to send Lelia to college in Knoxville, Tennessee.

Sarah had a reputation as a good laundress, but she wanted more for herself. "As I bent over the washboard and looked at my arms buried in the soapsuds, I said to myself, 'What are you going to do when you grow old and your back gets stiff?'" she later explained.[2] The answer to that question came to her after she prayed about another problem that was bothering her.

Because of stress and poor nutrition, Sarah's hair was dry and falling out. She had tried different hair care products, including those manufactured by the Poro Company, which specialized in products for black women's hair. These products did help, and for a while, Sarah worked for the company, selling Poro products door-to-door. However, they did not end her hair loss problem and she prayed for a solution. Her answer came in a dream. "One night I had a dream; a big Black man appeared to me and told me what to mix up for my hair," Sarah recalled.[3]

Some of the ingredients were available only in Africa, but she sent for them and mixed up her formula in a washtub. When she used the solution on herself, her hair began to grow back. She tried it on her friends and they also had good results. Sarah knew she had a product that many African-American women needed.

The Poro Company was already established in the St. Louis area, and Sarah did not want to compete with it. In July 1905, she moved to Denver. Her brother had died, but her sister-in-law and her nieces still lived in the area. The move meant that Sarah had to leave behind a good friend, Charles Joseph (C. J.) Walker. They agreed to keep in touch.

Sarah had only $1.50 in her pocket when she arrived in Denver. She got a job as a cook during the day. At night she worked on her hair care business. She developed three products—Vegetable Shampoo, Wonderful Hair Grower, and Glossine. She then began going door-to-door demonstrating her hair care method. She began by shampooing the customer's hair. Then she applied the hair grower, which promoted a healthy scalp. She finished with Glossine, a light oil that helped in styling the hair.

Charles Walker soon joined her in Denver. Their friendship grew into love, and on January 4, 1906, they were married. Sarah, now Mrs. Charles Joseph Walker, began calling herself Madam C. J. Walker. She thought Madam sounded better. The name appeared in advertisements that Walker used to sell her products by mail. Her husband, C. J., had experience as a newspaper salesman. He designed the ads, which showed before and after photos of Madam C. J. Walker.

In September 1906, Walker began an exhausting eighteen-month tour throughout the United States. By that time, her daughter, Lelia, had graduated from college and moved to Denver. She handled the mail-order part of the business while her mother traveled. During her travels, Walker sold her products, and she also trained other women in the Walker Hair Care Method. These women—Walker called them hair culturalists—received a commission for the products they sold. Earning a commission meant that instead of an hourly wage, they received a percentage of the money they took in on their sales of the products.

In 1908, Walker moved her business base to Pittsburgh, Pennsylvania. Pittsburgh was closer to cities such as New York City, Washington, D.C., and Baltimore, which had large African-American populations. Walker and her daughter founded Lelia Beauty College in Pittsburgh, where they trained women to become Walker agents.

Walker continued to travel while her daughter ran the beauty school. During a trip to Indianapolis, Indiana, Walker was impressed with the transportation system there. Because it was easy to get products in and out of the city, Walker decided to build a factory there. In 1910, Walker and her husband moved to Indianapolis. Her daughter remained in Pittsburgh.

Walker hired Alice Kelly as her factory forewoman. Kelly, who had been a teacher in Kentucky, also tutored Walker. Walker had always regretted her lack of a formal education, and she was eager to learn.

As Walker's business grew, it affected her marriage. Walker and her husband disagreed about expanding the business. Late in 1912, they were divorced. However, C. J. Walker continued to work for the company for the rest of his life.

In 1913, Walker's daughter, who had changed her name to A'Lelia, moved to the Harlem neighborhood of New York City. It was an exciting time to be living in Harlem, which was rapidly becoming an African-American cultural center. A'Lelia soon persuaded her mother to move there too. They lived in a townhouse, which included their living quarters and a beauty salon. Walker wore fine clothes and jewelry and she liked automobiles. She was often seen riding through the streets of Harlem in her fashionable modern automobile.

In 1918, Walker moved into a thirty-room mansion that she had built along the Hudson River in Irvington-on-Hudson, New York. The elaborate furnishings included a gold-plated grand piano and a huge pipe organ. Walker said that she built the mansion not only for herself, but also as an example to other African Americans of what they could achieve.

Walker enjoyed entertaining at the mansion and often hosted large parties.

Although Walker enjoyed her wealth, she was also generous with her earnings. She donated large sums of money to schools, YMCAs, children's homes, retirement homes, churches, and the National Association for the Advancement of Colored People (NAACP). "My object in life is not simply to make money for myself or to spend it on myself in dressing or running around in an automobile," she said,

Madam C. J. Walker was often seen behind the wheel of her automobile. She enjoyed the pleasures of her wealth, but she also made generous contributions to a variety of organizations.

"but I love to use a part of what I make in trying to help others."[4]

Walker continued to travel, giving speeches and opening beauty shops around the country, but her health was failing. She had high blood pressure and doctors warned her to slow down. She did not follow that advice. Walker died on May 25, 1919, of complications caused by her high blood pressure. She was fifty-one years old. In her will, Walker stated that only a woman could head her company. The Walker Company was sold in 1985, but Walker's hair care products are still available through Madam C. J. Walker Enterprises, Inc., in Indianapolis. Even under new ownership, a woman, Vivian Randolph, heads the company.

Walker helped other women become successful, not only by her example but also by giving them a way to be in business for themselves. By 1912, her agents earned twice as much as African-American women working at other jobs. "Madam Walker would have been pleased, but not surprised to see so many women in business today," Walker's great-great-granddaughter, A'Lelia P. Bundles, wrote in 1983. "It was exactly what she dreamed would happen and one of the things she worked so hard to achieve."[5]

Harriet Quimby

Harriet Quimby

Aviator

In 1911, airplanes were fragile machines and accident rates were high. People said the air was no place for a woman, but that did not discourage Harriet Quimby. That year she became the first American woman to earn a pilot's license. Eight months later, she was the first woman to fly across the English Channel.

Harriet Quimby was born on a farm near Coldwater, Michigan, on May 11, 1875. She was the second of William and Ursula Quimby's two daughters. In 1884, when Harriet was nine, the family moved to Arroyo Grande, California. William Quimby farmed there, and after the farm failed, he ran a general store. When that business also failed, Ursula Quimby took charge.

They moved to San Francisco, where Ursula Quimby and her daughters began mixing and packaging herbal medicine remedies in their home. William Quimby sold the products from a wagon. Ursula Quimby and her daughters also sewed for local fruit packers, making sacks to hold prunes.

Harriet Quimby, who inherited her mother's independent spirit, decided on a career in journalism. Journalism was a field that was just opening up for women. The only qualification Quimby needed was to show that she could do the job. She began as a writer for the San Francisco *Dramatic Review*. Later, she also wrote for the *Call-Bulletin & Chronicle*, another publication based in San Francisco. She was a great observer and was able to turn ordinary events into interesting stories.

Her reputation as a journalist spread, and by 1902, editors on the East Coast were interested in her talents. In January 1903, she moved to New York City. She got a job as a drama critic for *Leslie's Weekly*, a well-known publication of the time. In 1906, she became *Leslie's* first travel correspondent and traveled all over the world in search of stories. She learned to use a camera and took photos to accompany her articles.

She was looking for an interesting story when she attended an auto race on Long Island, New York, in 1906. She persuaded one of the race car drivers to give her a ride in his car. Quimby enjoyed that experience so much that she learned to drive. At a time when it was unusual to see a woman behind the wheel of a car, she drove herself to her writing assignments.

Quimby was again looking for a story in 1910 when she attended a flying meet at Belmont Park on Long Island. She was impressed with John Moisant, a young pilot at the meet. He and his brother, Albert, ran a flight school, and Quimby persuaded them to let her enroll. John Moisant was killed in a flying accident before Quimby began her lessons. Albert Moisant kept the school open, and Quimby went ahead with her plans to learn to fly.

She began her lessons in April 1911, flying at dawn when the air was calm. She knew that if reporters found out that a woman was piloting a plane, there would be a lot of publicity. To avoid that, she kept her lessons a secret and wore a man's flight suit and a hood to conceal her identity.

Her secret did not last long. Rumors spread that a woman was learning to fly, and a *New York Times* reporter decided to check it out. His story about Harriet Quimby made the front page of the paper.

Quimby's first article about her experiences was published in the May 25, 1911, issue of *Leslie's Weekly*. At that time, the cockpit had not been invented and planes had no windshields. The pilot sat out in the open on a flimsy seat, which was fastened to the framework of the plane by wires. When the plane was speeding through the air, wind and dirt blew directly into the pilot's face. Goggles gave some protection, but in her article Quimby wrote about something even worse. "Not only the chassis of the machine, but all the fixtures are slippery with lubricating oil," she wrote, "and when the engine is speeded a shower of this oil is also thrown back directly into the driver's face."[1]

Quimby earned her pilot's license on August 2, 1911. She was the first American woman to become a licensed pilot and the second woman in the world to do so. A French woman, Raymonde de Laroche, earned her license in March 1910.

Quimby then joined the Moisant Exhibition Team and began participating in air shows and flying meets. Her first air show was on September 4, 1911, on Staten Island, New York. She set a record at that meet by becoming the first woman to make a night flight.

By that time, Quimby had adopted the stylish flight suit that attracted almost as much attention as her flying. With the help of a designer, Quimby created a purple satin one-piece suit with a monk-style hood. The suit had wide legs that were tucked into tall lace-up boots.

In November 1911, Quimby went to Mexico City, to perform with the Moisant Exhibition Team. While she was in Mexico, she decided what her next challenge would be. She wanted to become the first woman to fly across the English Channel.

Quimby's historic flight began in the early morning hours of April 16, 1912. Her plane was wheeled onto the runway in Dover, located on the southeastern coast of England. From there she planned to fly across the channel to Calais, France. It was a twenty-two-mile trip, quite a distance for a flight at that time, especially in a plane that she had never flown. It would also be Quimby's first flight over water. Her only navigational equipment was a compass. Quimby had never used a compass before, but just before takeoff she got a few hurried instructions on how to use it. She was dressed in several layers of clothing to protect her from the cold. She also had a hot water bottle tied around her waist for extra warmth.

Quimby took off at 5:30 A.M. and quickly ran into problems when she flew into dense fog. "I could not see ahead of me at all nor could I see the water below," she recalled. "There was only one thing for me to do and that was to keep my eyes fixed on the compass."[2] She knew that if she veered five miles off course to the north, she would be over the North Sea, an area where other pilots had lost their lives.

Moisture from the fog collected on her goggles and Quimby could not see. She finally pushed her goggles to her forehead, which created another problem. "I was traveling at a mile a minute and the mist felt like tiny needles on my skin," she recalled.[3]

Quimby finally saw land, but she could not find Calais. Instead, she flew along the coast until she found a place on the beach where she could land. She set down about two miles outside the town of Hardelot, about twenty-five miles south of Calais.

Harriet Quimby cranks the motor of her plane. For her own safety, she was in the habit of checking her plane before each flight.

Quimby did not get the recognition she deserved for her historic flight. The ocean liner *Titanic* hit an iceberg and had sunk in the North Atlantic just one day earlier, on April 15. The day after Quimby's flight, news about the survivors of the *Titanic* was just becoming available. Newspapers were filled with stories about that tragedy. The article about Quimby's flight was buried on page eighteen of *The New York Times*.

Quimby continued to fly in air shows, but she did not do the dangerous stunts that some pilots performed. Quimby's hope was that people would accept flight as the transportation of the future. "The time is coming when we shall find the means of transportation by bird-like flights as safe and satisfactory as transportation by steamship or locomotive and with still greater speed," she predicted. "This is not to be accomplished by racing or doing circus tricks in the air at aviation meets."[4] To ensure her own safety, Quimby was in the habit of checking her own aircraft before each flight.

On July 1, 1912, Quimby was participating in the Harvard-Boston Aviation Meet at Squantum Airfield in Boston, Massachusetts. She was flying a two-seated Bleriot plane. The second seat, for a passenger, was directly behind the pilot's seat. Both the pilot and the passenger sat out in the open without even a windshield for protection. Many people thought the plane was too dangerous to fly with a passenger because if the passenger shifted his weight the plane became unstable. When no passengers were on board, a sandbag was strapped to the rear seat to balance the plane.

Normally, Quimby did not take passengers. On that day, though, she agreed to take William Willard, the air show manager, for a practice flight over the course. They had dropped to about one thousand feet, getting ready to come in for a landing, when the plane took a sudden dip. Horrified onlookers watched as Willard was tossed from the plane. It appeared that Quimby regained control of the plane, but then it dipped again and she was flung from her seat and fell to her death. The plane, which came out of its dive and glided to a stop, showed very little damage.

There was disagreement over what caused the accident. Some people thought that Quimby hit an air pocket. Others suspected that Willard had leaned forward to talk to Quimby. The sudden shift in weight caused the plane to become unstable. Others said that it was pilot error and used the accident as an example of why women should not be allowed to fly. It was ironic that Quimby, who believed in the safety of flight, died because of a safety feature that was not yet required on planes. Experts later said that neither Willard nor Quimby would have died if they had been wearing seat belts.

At the time of her death, Quimby had already made plans for another first. She was scheduled to fly a bag of mail nonstop from Boston to New York on July 7, the last day of the Harvard-Boston Aviation Meet.

Quimby predicted great futures for women pilots. "In my opinion there is no reason why the aeroplane should not open a fruitful occupation for women," she wrote shortly before her death. "I see no reason why they cannot realize handsome incomes by carrying passengers between adjacent towns, why they cannot derive incomes from parcel delivery, from taking photographs from above, or from conducting schools for flying."[5] Her predictions have all come true.

Jeannette Rankin

Jeannette Rankin

U.S. Congresswoman

In the early morning hours of April 6, 1917, the galleries in the U.S. House of Representatives were overflowing with observers. All eyes were on Jeannette Rankin, the thirty-six-year-old Republican representative from Montana. President Woodrow Wilson had asked Congress to declare war on Germany. The Senate had already given its approval. Now, after sixteen hours of debate lasting well past midnight, members of the House were casting their votes.

Rankin did not believe in war, and people wondered how she would vote. When her name was called, she stood and said, "I want to stand by my country, but I cannot vote for war."[1] Forty-nine other representatives voted against war that day. However, it was Rankin's vote that got the most attention, for she was the first woman ever to serve in Congress.

Rankin was born in Montana Territory on June 11, 1880, nine years before Montana became a state. She was the oldest of John and Olive Rankin's seven children.

Until Jeannette was five, the family lived on a ranch about six miles outside the town of Missoula. Then they moved into a house that John Rankin built in town. They also kept their ranch, and for the next several years, Jeannette spent the harsh Montana winters in their house in town and summers on the ranch.

Jeannette looked forward to summers and exploring on the ranch. She liked to ride, and she learned how to care for the horses, too. Once, when she was about twelve, a hired hand rode in on a horse that had been cut by a barbed wire fence. Jeannette ran into the house, got her sewing kit and hot water, and cleaned and stitched the horse's wound herself.

Jeannette thought school was boring, and she was in a hurry to move on to more exciting activities. "Go! Go! Go!" a teenaged Rankin wrote in her journal.[2] She had the urge to do *something*, but she was not sure what. By the time she graduated from high school, the University of Montana was opening in Missoula, and she enrolled. She majored in biology, graduating in 1902 with a bachelor of science (B.S.) degree.

About the only thing her degree had prepared her for was teaching. She tried it for a couple of years but never got a permanent teaching certificate. She also tried dressmaking and furniture design, but she could not find a career that challenged her. The traditional role for women at that time was marriage and raising a family. Rankin had marriage proposals, but she turned them down and continued her search for fulfilling work. That search took her to San Francisco, where she lived and worked at a settlement house known as the Telegraph Hill Association. Her experience there convinced her that she wanted to become a social worker.

In 1908, she enrolled at the New York School of Philanthropy (which later became the Columbia University School of Social Work) in New York City. After graduation, she returned to Missoula, but found there was little opportunity for a social worker there. In 1910, she accepted a position at a children's home in Spokane, Washington. She quit that job after only a few weeks, dissatisfied with the way the home was managed. She then enrolled at the University of Washington in Seattle, where her studies included courses in public speaking.

At that time, most women in the United States could not vote. However, some states were passing legislation that gave women in those states that right. That fall, voters in the state of Washington were set to decide the issue of woman suffrage—the right to vote—and Rankin got involved. She traveled all over the state putting up posters and giving speeches.

Women in Washington won the right to vote on November 3, 1910.

Spurred on by that success, Rankin turned her attention to woman suffrage in her home state, Montana. Early in 1912, the Montana legislature was going to decide if the issue should be put to voters in the November election. Rankin asked to address the members of the Montana House of Representatives on behalf of woman suffrage. It was the first time a woman had spoken before the Montana House.

It appeared that Rankin made a good impression on the legislators, for the majority of them voted to put woman suffrage on the ballot. Unfortunately, a two-thirds majority was needed, and they were two votes short of that goal. Even so, it was encouraging that the vote was so close.

Rankin went on to work for woman suffrage in New York, California, Ohio, and Wisconsin. In 1913, she became field secretary for the National American Woman Suffrage Association. In that role, she traveled all over the United States speaking about woman suffrage. She also continued to work for woman suffrage in Montana. In 1914, Montana became the tenth state to give women the right to vote.

Rankin decided that the next step was for women to have a representative in Congress. In 1916, she ran for one of two at-large seats in Montana for the U.S. House of Representatives. She ran on a platform that included working for a constitutional amendment to give all women the right to vote. Another part of her platform was to keep the United States out of war. Voters agreed with her. World War I was already raging in Europe, but Americans did not want to get involved. Rankin won that election by more than seven thousand votes. She became the first woman elected to Congress at a time when most women in the United States could not even vote.

By the time Rankin took her seat in the House on April 2, 1917, Americans had changed their minds about not getting involved in the war. German submarines had attacked American ships, and Americans felt that they needed to act. Rankin's first important vote in the House was whether or not to declare war on Germany.

Rankin struggled with her conscience. As a pacifist she was against war, but she knew that if she voted no, people would be angry with her. Friends urged her to vote with the majority. After all, her vote would not be a deciding one. But when the time came, Rankin followed her conscience. Her brother, who was also her political advisor, was furious with her. He said that her vote had ruined her political future. "You know you're not going to be reelected," he said.[3]

Others were just as angry. "Is the first woman in Congress a failure?" one of her constituents wrote.[4] A Presbyterian minister called for her resignation. *The New York Times* questioned her judgment, and woman suffragists cancelled her speaking engagements in their behalf.

In the meantime, Rankin went on with the business of being a U.S. representative. The majority had voted for war and now the right thing to do was to support that effort. She gave speeches urging people to buy Liberty Bonds, which were sold to earn money for the war effort. She also voted in favor of other legislative issues relating to the war. During her term in Congress, she worked on legislation to improve working conditions for women. She also served on a committee that wrote a first draft of the Nineteenth Amendment to the Constitution, giving all women the right to vote. That amendment passed in 1920, but by that time, Rankin was no longer a member of Congress.

Redistricting in Montana had eliminated the at-large seats for the House of Representatives. Since Rankin could not run a statewide campaign for the House, she decided to run for the Senate, but she failed to get elected.

For the next few years, Rankin devoted much of her time to working for peace. In 1923, she bought land near Athens, Georgia, where she founded the Georgia Peace Society in 1928. The purpose of this organization was to educate people about peace. In 1929, she went to work for the National Council for the Prevention of War, which was the largest and most active organization for peace in the United States.

Jeannette Rankin addresses the National American Woman Suffrage Association in Washington, D.C., in 1917, the year she became the first woman elected to Congress. Behind her is Carrie Chapman Catt, president of the suffrage association.

In 1939, World War II was approaching. Rankin, who was then fifty-nine years old, decided to run for a House seat from Montana, where she still maintained a residence. Once again, Americans did not want to get involved in a foreign war and Rankin was elected to the House as a representative for peace.

Then, on December 7, 1941, Japan bombed the U.S. naval base at Pearl Harbor, Hawaii, and public opinion changed. In a strange twist of history, the candidate who had been elected to Congress as a pacifist was once again being asked to vote for war. This time the debate in the House was a short one, lasting less than an hour. Rankin was the only member of Congress to vote against war. Her vote was followed by boos from other members of the House. Outside, mobs of people waited for her and she needed police protection to get back to her office. She said her vote was meant as a statement against the violence of war. "I voted against it because it was war," she explained.[5]

Rankin had no hope of being reelected and she retired from politics when her term ended. She stayed out of the public eye until 1968, when she organized the Jeannette Rankin Brigade. This was a group of five thousand women who marched down Pennsylvania Avenue to Capitol Hill on January 15 as a protest against U.S. involvement in the Vietnam War. Rankin was then eighty-seven years old. Later, Rankin considered running for Congress again as a representative for peace, but poor health kept her from carrying out that plan.

Rankin died on May 18, 1973, at the age of ninety-two. On May 1, 1985, a bronze life-sized statue of Rankin was placed in the Capitol Rotunda in Washington, D.C. Hers was the ninety-fourth statue placed in that gallery. It was the sixth statue of a woman.

Rankin saw a future for women in Congress. In a 1966 interview she said, "We're half the people; we should be half the Congress."[6] Although that goal is far from being reached, by the end of the twentieth century, 177 women had joined Rankin in being elected to the House of Representatives.

Frances Perkins

Frances Perkins

Secretary of Labor

On March 6, 1933, Frances Perkins began work as U.S. Secretary of Labor. She was the first woman to become a member of a president's cabinet, and it could not have come at a worse time. The United States was then in the midst of the economic crisis known as the Great Depression. Banks closed, factories and businesses shut down, and people who had once had good jobs were unemployed and living in poverty. Perkins had a hard job ahead of her, and she knew it.

Frances, the daughter of Fred and Susie Perkins, was born in Boston, Massachusetts, on April 10, 1880. When she was two, the family moved to

Worcester, Massachusetts, where her father ran a stationery store.

Fred Perkins was a scholarly person who had little time for idle chatter. He taught Frances to be brief. When she talked too much, he rapped on the table and said, "Don't waste people's time with vaporings. If you have anything to say, say it definitely and stop."[1]

Frances spent summers with her widowed grandmother on the family farm in Newcastle, Maine. Her grandmother was a great influence on her life. "Scarcely a week goes by that I don't find myself saying, 'As my grandmother used to say,' and then repeating something that apparently has been a guiding principle all of my life," Perkins recalled.[2]

Frances attended Worcester Classical High School, where most of her classmates were boys. She graduated from high school on June 20, 1898, and enrolled at Mount Holyoke College, a women's college in South Hadley, Massachusetts.

Perkins's classmates called her "Perk" and said she had a great sense of humor. She performed in college plays and was elected senior class president. She said that her teachers at Mount Holyoke taught her to think. "I discovered for the first time . . . that I had a mind," she recalled.[3] She majored in chemistry and physics, graduating in 1902.

She spent the next two years teaching in the Worcester area. Then, in 1904, she moved to Lake Forest, Illinois. There she taught high school science at Ferry Hall, a distinguished girls' school. In her spare time, Perkins volunteered at Jane Addams's Hull House in Chicago. Working among Chicago's poor convinced her to make a career change. She decided to go into social work.

In the fall of 1907, Perkins got a job at the Philadelphia Research and Protective Association. Young immigrant women and young black women from the South had moved to the Philadelphia area to work. There were reports that employers were treating these women poorly. Perkins's job was to investigate the reports and to develop programs to help these women.

While she was working in Philadelphia, she took night courses in social work at the University of Pennsylvania. She then earned a scholarship to study at Columbia University in New York City. She received her master's degree in social work from Columbia in 1910.

Perkins then went to work for the New York City branch of the National Consumers' League. This organization was founded in 1899 to inspect and investigate factories and work for legislation to improve factory conditions. Perkins worked for child labor laws and for passage of the 54-hour bill. This bill limited the number of hours that women and children could be required to work each week. She also investigated safety conditions in factories. At that time safety equipment was not required on machines. Factories were overcrowded, lighting was poor, and employees worked long hours. As a result, the accident rate was high.

Fire safety was another problem. Many factories were located on the top floors of a building, out of the reach of the extension ladders on fire trucks of the time. Sprinkler systems were not required and there were not enough exits for the number of people working in the factories. This issue got more public attention after a fire at the Triangle Shirtwaist Company in New York City on March 25, 1911. There was only one fire escape and it quickly became too hot to use. Other exits had been locked earlier by the employers, and the workers were trapped.

When the fire broke out, Perkins was nearby having tea with friends. She ran out into the street, where she saw young women with their clothes on fire, jumping from the windows. Tragically, they died from the fall. One hundred forty-six young women died in that fire and Perkins never forgot what she saw. "I felt I must sear it not only on my mind but on my heart as a never-to-be-forgotten reminder of why I had to spend my life fighting conditions that could permit such a tragedy," she said.[4]

After the fire, two committees were formed to make factories safer. Citizens of New York City formed the Committee on Safety of the City of New York. The New York State Factory Investigating Commission was formed by the New York state legislature. Perkins served as an advisor to both of these groups. In 1912, she resigned from her position at the National Consumers' League and went to work full-time for the Committee on Safety.

Perkins married Paul Wilson on September 26, 1913. Going against tradition, she kept her maiden name, which drew some criticism. Perkins was often forced to explain that choice. Their daughter, Susanna, was born on December 30, 1916.

In 1919, Governor Alfred E. Smith asked Perkins to join the Industrial Commission of the State of New York. The Industrial Commission supervised factory inspectors, helped settle labor disputes, and made final decisions about workmen's compensation cases. Workmen's compensation is money paid to workers who are injured on the job. Many people protested Perkins's appointment. Traditionally, the members of the Industrial Commission were men who had backgrounds in organized labor, such as labor unions formed by workers to help and protect them in dealing with employers. However, the New York State Senate approved Perkins's appointment by a vote of thirty-four to sixteen.

On February 18, 1919, she became the first woman appointed to the Industrial Commission and the highest-paid state female employee in the country. By that time, Perkins was her family's main source of income. Her husband suffered mental health problems that caused him to be hospitalized often. He never again worked steadily.

In 1929, Franklin Delano Roosevelt was elected governor of New York. He promoted Perkins to industrial commissioner, the head of the New York State Department of Labor. That appointment made her a member of the governor's cabinet, another first for a woman.

On October 24, 1929, the stock market crashed, sending the country into its worse economic crisis, the Great Depression. Perkins immediately began talking about the need for unemployment insurance, something other countries already had. She also studied ways to decrease unemployment.

Roosevelt was elected president of the United States in 1932. He asked Perkins to become his secretary of labor. But Perkins had doubts. "I honestly felt that I was not the right person for the job," she later wrote.[5] Roosevelt persuaded her to accept, and she was sworn into office in March 1933.

Not everyone agreed with Perkins's appointment. William Green, president of the American Federation of Labor, said, "Labor can never become reconciled to the selection made."[6] However, those feelings changed once Perkins went to work.

She helped create programs to get unemployed Americans back to work. She worked for laws that set minimum wages and a maximum number of hours that employers could ask their employees to work. This legislation also gave employees the legal right to organize for better working conditions. She also worked on drafting the Social Security Act, which was approved by Congress on August 10, 1935. The Social

Secretary of Labor Frances Perkins looks on as President Franklin D. Roosevelt signs a bill creating the U.S. Employment Services. It was one of the many programs Perkins helped create to ease the United States out of the Great Depression.

Security Act provided for old age and unemployment insurance.

Perkins established herself as a friend to labor, but she also had critics. She was criticized for not being able to stop labor strikes. "I am aware that there is a theory that if I were a two-fisted male I should be able to stop strikes," she noted.[7]

Reporters labeled Perkins as being unfriendly because she would not talk about her private life. "We New Englanders like to keep ourselves to ourselves," she explained.[8]

Her worst crisis came when she refused to deport a strike leader. She was called a Communist and threatened with impeachment. However, the impeachment proceedings were dropped after Perkins testified before the House Judiciary Committee on February 8, 1939.

By 1940, Perkins was tired from the stress of being secretary of labor. She told Roosevelt that she wanted to resign. But when he asked her to stay on as secretary of labor, she did.

Perkins served as secretary of labor throughout Roosevelt's years as president. During that time, the country survived the Great Depression and fought in World War II. In 1944, Roosevelt was elected to a fourth term as president. He died on April 12, 1945, and Vice President Harry S. Truman became president. Perkins served another two months as secretary of labor under Truman. Spanning more than twelve years, hers was the second-longest cabinet term in history. Roosevelt's secretary of the interior, Harold

Ickes, served seven and a half months longer. In 1946, Perkins's biography of Roosevelt, *The Roosevelt I Knew*, was published.

Perkins intended to retire from public life, but President Truman asked her to serve on the Civil Service Commission. This agency is in charge of government workers. She held that position from 1945 to 1953. In 1957, at the age of seventy-seven, she accepted a position as professor at Cornell University's School of Industrial and Labor Relations. She taught at the university until two weeks before her death on May 14, 1965. She was eighty-five years old.

W. Willard Wirtz, who was then secretary of labor, paid tribute to Perkins and her accomplishments. "Every man and woman in America who works at a living wage, under safe conditions, for reasonable hours, or who is protected by unemployment insurance or social security is her debtor," he said.[9]

Pearl S. Buck

Pearl S. Buck

Winner of the Nobel Prize in Literature

Pearl S. Buck loved two countries—the United States, where she was born, and China, where she lived most of her first forty years. Her dream was to become a writer and to use her writing to promote understanding between the people of these two very different countries. She created an impressive collection of novels and biographies that earned her the Nobel Prize in literature in 1938. She was the first American woman to win that prize, one of the highest honors a writer can receive.

She was born Pearl Sydenstricker in Hillsboro, West Virginia, on June 26, 1892. Her parents, Absalom and Caroline Sydenstricker were missionaries in China. At the time of Pearl's birth, they were in the United States on a yearlong furlough, an extended vacation from their missionary work. They returned to China when baby Pearl was only a few months old.

Pearl's interest in writing began early. She was six years old when her first essay was published. It appeared in the "Letters to the Editor" section of the *Christian Observer,* a newspaper based in Louisville, Kentucky. In that article, Pearl wrote about the death of her four-year-old brother, Clyde. "On the tenth of last month my little brave brother, Clyde, left us to go to our real home in Heaven," she wrote.[1]

Pearl was encouraged by the publication of her first story. She followed with others that were published in the children's section of the *Shanghai Mercury.* That English-language newspaper was based in Shanghai, located on the eastern coast of China.

Pearl's parents were stationed in Chinkiang, a small city on the Yangtze River. The family lived in the Chinese community rather than in the area where most of the foreigners lived. Pearl played in the homes of her Chinese friends and learned to speak Chinese before she could speak English. "I had almost ceased to think of myself as different, if indeed I ever thought so, from the Chinese," she recalled.[2] But she was different and that became obvious in 1900 when Pearl was eight.

Some Chinese people were opposed to Western and Christian influences in their country. Secret societies were formed to fight these influences. The best known of these societies was called the Boxers. In the Boxer Rebellion of 1900, the Boxers and other secret societies attacked and killed Westerners and Chinese Christians. For their safety, Pearl, her mother, and Pearl's younger sister, Grace, sought refuge in Shanghai. From there they could sail to America if needed. Pearl's father stayed behind in Chinkiang. After a year in Shanghai, Pearl, her mother, and sister returned to Chinkiang.

When Pearl was fifteen, her parents sent her to the Jewell School, a boarding school in Shanghai. In 1910, she enrolled at Randolph-Macon Woman's College in Lynchburg, Virginia. In her final year of college, she entered a writing contest at the school. Awards were given for best short story and best poem. She won both categories.

She graduated in 1914 and accepted an offer to teach psychology at the college. She had taught only one semester when she received word that her mother was seriously ill. She returned to China, where she spent the next two years nursing her mother back to health. She also taught at a school for boys run by the mission board.

On May 30, 1917, Pearl married John Lossing Buck. He was an agriculturist whose goal was to teach modern farming methods to the Chinese. The Bucks moved to a poor rural area in northern China, where they lived for the next few years. Their daughter Carol was born in the spring of 1921. Then they moved to the city of Nanking, where Buck taught English literature at the University of Nanking.

That fall, Buck's mother died. As a way to deal with her mother's death, Buck began writing her mother's biography. When she finished the biography, she set it aside, but she continued writing. She wrote an essay titled "In China, Too," which was published in the *Atlantic Monthly*, an American magazine.

By the time Carol was a few years old, it was obvious that she was not developing normally. In 1924, the Bucks took a leave and sailed for America, where specialists could examine Carol. On the ship, Pearl Buck wrote during her daughter's naptimes. By the time they arrived in the United States, she had finished her first piece of fiction, a short story called "A Chinese Woman Speaks." That story was later published in *Asia Magazine*.

Buck had a busy year in the United States. She took Carol to several specialists, finally learning that Carol was severely mentally handicapped. Buck also enrolled at Cornell University in Ithaca, New York. In 1926, she earned a master's degree in literature from the university. The Bucks also adopted a baby girl, Janice. Later that year, the family returned to Nanking, China.

At that time, China was in the midst of civil war between Communist and Nationalist groups. In March 1927, the Bucks received word that Chinese revolutionaries had entered Nanking. They had already murdered a university official, and other white people were injured. For the second time in her life, Buck knew what it meant to fear for her life because of the color of her skin.

One of the Bucks' servants, Mrs. Lu, hid the Buck family in her hut. Mrs. Lu was putting her own life in danger. If the soldiers discovered that she was hiding Westerners in her home, she too would be killed. The Bucks spent fourteen tense hours huddled in Mrs. Lu's home before they were rescued by American troops. "The only reason that I was not killed was because my Chinese friends knew me under my skin and risked their lives for me," Buck recalled.[3]

The Bucks spent the next year in Japan. When they returned to China during the summer of 1928, they found that soldiers had looted their home. The novel that Buck had been working on was gone. Buck tried not to be discouraged. "Probably it was no good," she said.[4]

It was still a dangerous time for Westerners to live in China. Buck worried about Carol. If anything happened to her or her husband, Carol would not be able to understand or adjust to a new situation. Buck decided that it would be better for Carol to be in the United States. In 1929, Buck enrolled Carol at the Vineland Training School, a school for the mentally handicapped, in Vineland, New Jersey. Although she hated to leave her daughter behind, Buck returned to China.

The challenge to earn the money for her daughter's care at the school made Buck's writing more important to her than ever. Richard Walsh at the John Day Company in New York bought her first novel, *East Wind: West Wind*. It was published in 1930 when Buck was thirty-eight years old.

Her second novel, *The Good Earth*, made her famous. That novel tells the story of Wang Lung, a Chinese farmer. The setting is the rural farming area where Buck had spent the first three years of her marriage. She also used other events from her life in China. The book was published in March 1931 and quickly became a best-seller. In 1932, it won a Pulitzer Prize as the best American novel of 1931. It was made into a movie in 1937.

Buck wrote two more books about Wang Lung and his family—*Sons* (1932) and *A House Divided* (1935). Buck's writing was going well, but her marriage was not. It had never been a happy marriage. Buck and her husband had little in common. "I married a handsome face, and who wants to live with just a handsome face," she later said.[5] In 1934, Buck and her daughter Janice moved to the United States.

The Bucks divorced in 1935. That same year, Pearl Buck married her editor, Richard Walsh. They made their home on Green Hills Farm in Bucks County, Pennsylvania. Over the next few years, they adopted six children.

With the help of a full-time nurse to care for the children, Buck continued to write. In 1936, *The*

In 1934, after spending much of her life in China, Pearl S. Buck
moved back to the United States.

Exile, her biography of her mother, was published. She also wrote her father's biography, *Fighting Angel,* which was published in 1938. When the Nobel Prize committee chose to honor her in 1938, they said that the biographies had played an important part in her selection.

It was not easy being the first American woman to receive the Nobel Prize in literature. "I think I was a little hurt that so many men writers wrote against my receiving this prize, not only because I was a woman, but because they considered that I was not really American since I had been reared abroad and wrote about Asian people," Buck said.[6]

Buck is also known for her charitable works. In 1949, she founded Welcome House, an adoption agency for children of mixed Asian-American blood. She expanded this work through the Pearl S. Buck Foundation, founded in 1964. In addition to adoptions, this foundation provides support for Asian-American children who are not eligible for adoption.

Buck also worked to help the mentally handicapped, donating money for medical research. She wrote about her daughter Carol in an article published in the *Ladies' Home Journal* (May 1950). That same year it was published in book form as *The Child Who Never Grew.* Buck donated her earnings from the article and the book to the Vineland Training School.

With modern medical advances, it was discovered that Carol suffered from PKU syndrome. This condition prevents the body from using protein properly. Babies are now routinely checked for this condition at birth. With treatment, they are able to live normal lives.

Buck died of cancer on March 6, 1973, at the age of eighty. She was buried on Green Hills Farm. Buck wrote eighty-five books, including children's novels and her autobiography, *My Several Worlds* (1954). Green Hills Farm is now a National Historic Landmark and headquarters for the Pearl S. Buck Foundation, which continues the work she began.

Althea Gibson

Althea Gibson
Tennis Champion

Growing up in New York City on the streets of Harlem, Althea Gibson did not seem like a future champion. She was rebellious, always getting into fights and skipping school. It was tennis that helped turn her life around.

She began taking lessons in 1941 and quickly became a star player with the American Tennis Association (ATA), an African-American sports association. However, she was not allowed to play in tournaments sponsored by the leading amateur organization, the United States Lawn Tennis Association (USLTA). Those tournaments were played at exclusive all-white country clubs. In 1950, Gibson became the first player to cross that color barrier. By 1957, she was ranked number one in the world in women's singles.

Althea Gibson was born on August 25, 1927, in Silver, South Carolina. When she was three, her parents, Daniel and Annie Gibson, moved north. They settled in the Harlem neighborhood of New York City.

Althea was the oldest child in a family that later grew to include three more girls and a boy. She said she was also the most difficult child. She did not like rules—and that included being told that she had to go to school. She often played hooky, preferring to spend her days playing basketball or baseball, or going bowling or to the movies. "I just wanted to play, play, play," Gibson recalled. "My mother would send me out with money for bread, and I'd be out from morning to dark—and not bring home the bread."[1] After one year of high school, Althea dropped out.

She floated from job to job, spending time as a counter girl at a restaurant, an elevator operator, a mail clerk, and a factory worker. She even cleaned chickens at a butcher shop for a while.

It was Buddy Walker, a musician who spent summers working for the city's recreation department, who got her started in tennis. Walker saw Gibson playing paddle tennis in Harlem, where she was the paddle tennis champion. Paddle tennis is similar to tennis except that it is played with a smaller wooden racket on a court about half the size of a regular tennis court. Walker gave Gibson a used tennis racket and arranged for her to practice with one of his friends.

Walker's friend cleared the way for Gibson to play at the Cosmopolitan Tennis Club, an upscale club in Harlem. Club members, who recognized Gibson's athletic ability, chipped in to pay her membership fees. They also paid for her to take lessons with the club's pro, a professional instructor.

Althea knew that she had more to learn about tennis than how to hit the ball. She also had to learn the manners of the game. "I had trouble as a competitor because I kept wanting to fight the other player every time I started to lose a match," she recalled. "But I could see that certain things were expected, in fact required, in the way of behavior on a tennis court, and I made up my mind that I would go along with the program."[2]

A year after starting lessons, she played in her first tournament—a New York State Open championship sponsored by the ATA. She won that tournament, and later that summer entered her first national tournament, losing in the finals. She won the girls' singles at the ATA national championships in 1944 and again in 1945.

In 1946, Gibson turned eighteen, which qualified her to play in the ATA national women's singles tournament. Although she lost in the finals, she did attract the attention of two African-American doctors—Dr. Hubert A. Eaton of Wilmington, North

Carolina, and Dr. Robert W. Johnson of Lynchburg, Virginia. Both of them were active in the ATA.

Although they did not tell Gibson at the time, they were looking for a player who could break the color barrier in tennis. They thought that she might be the one. They made an arrangement with Gibson to cover her living expenses so that she could get an education and continue playing tennis.

During the school year, she lived in Wilmington with Dr. Eaton and his family. She attended school, where she was placed in the tenth grade. After school, she practiced her tennis game on Eaton's private court in his backyard. During the summer, she lived with the Johnson family in Lynchburg and traveled the tennis circuit with Dr. Johnson.

During her first summer on the tennis circuit in 1947, Gibson played in nine tournaments. She won the women's singles division in all of them. She and Dr. Johnson also topped the mixed-doubles division in eight of those tournaments. The highlight of the summer was when Gibson won the ATA women's singles championship. She continued to win this title every year after that until she quit playing the tournament in 1957.

Gibson had also decided to take her studies seriously. When she graduated from high school in June 1949, she was ranked tenth in her class academically. She received an athletic scholarship to attend college at Florida Agricultural and Mechanical College (Florida A&M) at Tallahassee.

That summer Gibson played in two USLTA indoor events. She made it to the quarterfinals of both of those tournaments. Although she was allowed to participate in those indoor events, she was not invited to play in the USLTA's prestigious summer grass tournaments. These tournaments were played at all-white country clubs, such as the West Side Tennis Club in Forest Hills, New York, and the All-England Club in Wimbledon, England.

It was tennis champion Alice Marble who brought attention to the unfairness of that situation. Marble, who was white, wrote an editorial for *American Lawn Tennis,* which appeared in the July 1950 issue. "I've never met Miss Gibson but, to me, she is a fellow human being to whom equal privileges ought to be extended," Marble wrote.[3]

Marble's editorial opened doors for Gibson. For the first time, she was allowed to play in the USLTA-sponsored tournaments that qualified players for the National Championship at Forest Hills. On August 28, 1950, she became the first black person to play at Forest Hills. She lost in the second round of that tournament.

Gibson became a familiar face at USLTA tournaments over the next few years. She was tall and muscular and played a powerful game. "People thought I was ruthless, which I was," she later said. "I didn't give a darn who was on the other side of the net. I'd knock you down if you got in the way."[4] But she did not rise to become the champion that others had hoped she would be. Some said it was because she lacked confidence.

In 1953, she graduated from Florida A&M with a degree in physical education. She then accepted a teaching position in the physical education department at Lincoln University in Jefferson City, Missouri.

Her tennis career continued to be disappointing. By 1955, she was thinking about quitting tennis. Then she was selected as one of four American players to represent the United States on a goodwill tour through Asia. The tour was sponsored by the U.S. State Department.

The tour appeared to be the spark that ignited Gibson's tennis game. In 1956, she played in tournaments in Sweden, Germany, France, Italy, and Egypt. Then she went to Wimbledon, a tournament that many players call the world championship. She lost in the quarterfinals. However, she had participated in eighteen tournaments that season, winning sixteen of them. Because of her overall play, she was ranked second in the United States.

In 1957, Gibson won the National Championship in Forest Hills and then became the first black person to win at Wimbledon. She was ranked number one, and the Associated Press named her the 1957 Female Athlete of the Year. She successfully defended her titles at both Forest Hills and Wimbledon in 1958. Once again, she was named Female Athlete of the Year.

Althea Gibson was tall and muscular and played a powerful game of
tennis. In 1957, she became the first black person to win at Wimbledon.

Then, in a surprising move, Gibson announced her retirement. At that time, tennis was an amateur sport and players did not receive money for winning tournaments. They had to rely on benefactors—people who paid for their tournament expenses and gave them spending money. "Being a champ is all well and good," Gibson later wrote, "but you can't eat a crown."[5]

For the next few years, Gibson explored a variety of opportunities. She wrote her autobiography, *I Always Wanted to Be Somebody*, which was published in 1958. In 1959, she also recorded an album, *Althea Gibson Sings*, and had a small part in the movie *The Horse Soldiers*. The following year, she toured with the Harlem Globetrotters basketball team. She played tennis exhibition matches either before the games or during halftime. By 1962, she decided to try the professional golf circuit.

Gibson had begun playing golf in the 1950s. But golf, like tennis, was segregated. The Ladies Professional Golf Association (LPGA) tournaments were played at all-white country clubs. Gibson got support from Lennie Wirtz, the LPGA director. He said that it was time the golf courses accepted everyone. But it was up to Gibson to prove that she was good enough to earn her LPGA player's card. She did that in 1964 by finishing in the top 80 percent of the players in three tournaments. She became the first black player to hold an LPGA player's card. She spent seven years on the golf circuit, and then retired.

Gibson, with cowriter Richard Curtis, wrote another book, which was published in 1968. In that book, *So Much to Live For*, she talked about her years since she had retired from tennis. In 1971, she was inducted into the International Tennis Hall of Fame. She was honored again in 1980, when she became a member of the International Women's Sports Hall of Fame. After retiring from golf, Gibson spent the next twenty years teaching tennis. Gibson had to give up sports after a series of strokes left her partially paralyzed, but her story continues to inspire other athletes.

Justice Sandra Day O'Connor

Sandra Day O'Connor

U.S. Supreme Court Justice

On September 25, 1981, Sandra Day O'Connor was sworn in as a U.S. Supreme Court justice. Since the Court's creation in 1789, one hundred and one justices had sat on its bench. O'Connor was the first woman.

President Ronald Reagan was fulfilling a campaign promise when he nominated a woman to the Supreme Court. However, his reasons for selecting O'Connor went well beyond the fact that she was a woman. O'Connor's background included experience in both the legislative and judicial branches of government. It meant that she had experience in making laws as well as interpreting them. She was known as a woman who always did her homework and who looked at all sides of an issue before coming to a decision. All of those abilities would serve her well as a Supreme Court justice.

Sandra Day O'Connor was born on March 26, 1930, in El Paso, Texas, and grew up on her family's Lazy B ranch, located on the Arizona–New Mexico border. The ranch covered almost two hundred thousand acres, and the nearest town of any real size was twenty-five miles away.

For the first eight years of her life, Sandra was Harry and Ada Mae Day's only child. Then her sister, Ann, was born, followed by a brother, Alan, a year later.

Sandra's father taught her how to ride a horse, shoot a rifle, brand cows, and drive a tractor. When Sandra was only four years old, her mother taught her to read. Sandra's parents thought that it would be hard for her to get a good education in such an isolated area. When Sandra was six years old, they sent her to live with her maternal grandparents in El Paso, where she attended Radford School for Girls.

Sandra was close to her grandmother, even more so after her grandfather died when Sandra was in third grade. Still, Sandra was homesick in El Paso. Because of the distance, she was able to go home only for long holidays and summer vacations. "She'd always hide when it was time to go back," her father recalled.[1]

Sandra skipped a grade in elementary school and began attending Austin High School in El Paso a year early. She was able to complete her high school credits in three years and was only sixteen years old when she graduated.

Sandra applied for admission to only one college—Stanford University in Palo Alto, near San Francisco, California. It was the school her father had planned to attend, but he gave up that dream to take over the ranch after his father died. Sandra participated in a special program at Stanford that allowed students pursuing a career in law to complete their education in six years rather than the usual seven. Academically, she was ranked third in her class when she graduated in 1952.

In spite of her academic success, she had a hard time finding a job. "I interviewed with law firms in Los Angeles and San Francisco, but none had ever hired a woman before as a lawyer, and they were not prepared to do so," she recalled.[2] She did get a job as a law clerk in the San Mateo county attorney's office in California. She was quickly promoted to deputy county attorney.

In December 1952, she married John Jay O'Connor III. They had met when they were both law students at Stanford University. John O'Connor graduated from Stanford in the spring of 1953. He was soon drafted into the Army and sent to serve in Germany. Sandra Day O'Connor left her job at the county attorney's office and went to Germany with her husband. She worked as a civilian lawyer for the Army.

The O'Connors spent three years in Germany. Then John O'Connor got his discharge and they returned to the United States. In 1957, they settled in Phoenix, Arizona. John O'Connor landed a job with a good law firm in Phoenix. Their son Scott was born on October 8, 1957. Sandra O'Connor says law firms at that time were not interested in hiring a woman with a young child. O'Connor and a friend, Tom Tobin, decided to open their own law firm. O'Connor worked mornings and spent the afternoons at home with her small son.

The O'Connors' second son, Brian, was born in 1960. Sandra Day O'Connor then decided to stop working for a few years. Two years later, she had another son, Jay. While O'Connor was a full-time homemaker from 1960 to 1965, she was very involved in the community. She was a school and hospital volunteer and an advisor to the Salvation Army. She volunteered at the YWCA and a local historical society. She was also an active member of the Republican Party.

In 1965, she accepted a part-time job as an assistant attorney general for the state of Arizona. After her busy schedule as a volunteer, she said, "I decided I needed a paid job so that my life would be more orderly."[3]

Four years later, when a Republican-held seat in Arizona's state Senate became vacant, Republican Party leaders appointed O'Connor to finish out that term. She was elected to that position in 1970, and reelected in 1972. In her second term, the Republicans in the Senate selected her to become the Senate majority leader. The majority leader is the head of the political party with the most seats in the Senate. O'Connor was the first woman in the country to serve as majority leader in a state senate.

In 1974, O'Connor decided to return to law, running for a judge's seat on the Maricopa County Superior Court. At that time, voters were upset with the crime rate in Phoenix. O'Connor campaigned on a promise to get tough on crime. She was successful in defeating the current judge, who was running for reelection.

O'Connor lived up to her campaign promise. In fact, some people thought she was too tough. An example was the case of a woman who had written $3,500 in bad checks. The woman's husband had abandoned her and left her to care for their two small children. When her business failed, the woman became desperate and wrote the checks. People were shocked when O'Connor sentenced the woman to five to ten years in prison. However, O'Connor said that people had to be responsible for their actions.

O'Connor was always prepared for each case and expected the lawyers who were arguing cases before her to be prepared as well. Twice she told defendants in her court that they should get new lawyers because the ones they had were not doing their job.

In 1978, Arizona Republicans urged O'Connor to run for governor, but she decided against it.

Democrat Bruce Babbitt was elected governor that year. He later appointed O'Connor to a seat on the Arizona Court of Appeals. After a trial, if the defendants have reason to believe that they were not treated fairly, they can appeal the decision. The case is heard by a court of appeals. O'Connor's job was to decide either to uphold the previous ruling or to overturn it.

Two years later, President Ronald Reagan nominated O'Connor to the Supreme Court to replace Justice Potter Stewart, who was retiring. On September 22, 1981, the U.S. Senate approved her nomination with a vote of 99–0. (One senator did not vote.) At fifty-one years old, she became the youngest member of the Supreme Court.

O'Connor was surprised at the response from other women about her appointment. "I had no idea when I was appointed how *much* it would mean to many people around the country. It affected them in a very personal way—people saw the appointment as a signal that there are virtually unlimited opportunities for women," she said.[4]

One of the first things she did when she began her work on the Supreme Court was to organize an early-morning aerobics class for female employees of the Court. "I'm more productive with my work when I feel good physically," she said.[5] She also plays golf and tennis and enjoys skiing.

O'Connor experienced her own personal health crisis when she was diagnosed with breast cancer in

Supreme Court Justice Sandra Day O'Connor chats with President
Ronald Reagan on the White House patio in 1981. President Reagan
nominated Sandra Day O'Connor for the Supreme Court in 1980.

1988. She was back at work ten days after surgery. Her surgery was followed by chemotherapy treatment. She knew that the treatments would make her sick to her stomach and weak, so she scheduled her chemotherapy appointments on Fridays. That way she did not have to miss time at work. Since her battle with cancer, O'Connor has become a regular participant in the Race for the Cure, a fund-raiser for breast cancer research.

As a Supreme Court justice, O'Connor is known as a conservative. She is unlikely to vote for decisions involving big, sweeping changes. On the other hand, she is also known as an independent thinker, and it is hard to predict how she will rule on a case. On a panel of nine judges, she has often cast a deciding vote.

O'Connor has received thousands of letters from women who say that she has been an inspiration to them. Some of the letters include photos of little girls dressed in judge's robes—girls who hope to one day follow in her footsteps.

Marlene Sanders

Newswoman

Marlene Sanders made history in 1964 when she became the first woman to anchor a nighttime news show for a major television network. Two years later she became the first woman in broadcasting to cover the war in Vietnam. In 1976, she was the first woman to be named a vice president at a major network. In spite of those achievements, it would be many years before women became regulars on the evening news.

Sanders was born in Cleveland, Ohio, on January 10, 1931. She was the only child of Mac and Evelyn Ruth Sanders. They were divorced when Marlene was about a year old. Both of her parents remarried, which gave Marlene three half brothers.

Marlene Sanders

Growing up in the 1940s, Marlene learned that society expected young women to become good wives and mothers. They were not encouraged to work outside their homes. However, it was okay for a young woman to have a career to fall back on in case she never got married or something happened to her husband. Two professions that were considered good for women were teaching and nursing.

Marlene was not interested in either of those choices. "I knew that the traditional role was not going to be enough for me," Sanders said. "I had ambitions. I was going to be a great something—that something kept changing."[1]

Marlene enjoyed writing, and one of her teachers at Shaker Heights High School got her interested in politics. She also liked acting and was involved in children's theater in nearby Cleveland. By the time she graduated from high school in 1948, she had decided to become an actress.

She enrolled as a speech major at Ohio State University. Sanders left college for financial reasons after only one year. But she did not give up on her dream to become an actress. She spent the next two years studying acting at theaters, first in Cleveland and then in Philadelphia.

In June 1952, Sanders married her longtime boyfriend, Samuel Kahn. They moved to New York City, where Kahn enrolled at Columbia University and Sanders tried to make it on Broadway. She worked at temporary jobs and spent the rest of her time going to auditions. She did get a part in one off-Broadway play, but her acting career never really took off.

Her marriage was not working out either. She and her husband were divorced in 1955. "It took me two years to realize it was the wrong professional choice, and that my marriage was also a mistake," Sanders later wrote. "At twenty-four I had to make a fresh start."[2]

Sanders got a job as an assistant to the producer at a summer theater in Rhode Island. There she met an actor named Mike Wallace. He was producing one of the plays featured at the theater that summer, but he already had another job lined up for the fall. He was set to begin anchoring a television newscast on WABD-TV (later WNEW-TV) in New York City. This was something new. Until then, television stations did not have local news programs. WABD was the first to offer two fifteen-minute news shows—7:00 P.M. and 11:00 P.M.—five nights a week.

Sanders got in on the ground floor of this experiment when Wallace introduced her to Ted Yates, Jr., the producer of the newscast. Yates hired Sanders to be Wallace's production assistant. Sanders soon learned that her job as production assistant was to do whatever needed to be done. "Our newsroom was so low budget that we didn't even have a secretary," she recalled.[3]

Sanders worked long hours, but she says her early years in the news were some of the best in her career.

"The news department was small, everyone was friendly and learning the ropes together, and your whole career wasn't at stake every minute," she said.[4] That was because at that time there were no ratings battles. No one expected the news to make money. It was offered as a public service.

In 1956, Wallace and Yates began *Night Beat,* a late-night show on WNEW. It was a nightly interview show with famous personalities as guests. Sanders was hired to work on the show and was soon promoted to associate producer. Part of her job was to arrange for the guests on the show. "I became fearless on the phone," she recalled.[5]

Sanders was not always able to book the guests she went after. One of the people she failed to get was a symphony orchestra conductor. However, she did meet the orchestra's manager, Jerome Toobin. That meeting led to romance. After a short courtship, Sanders and Toobin married on May 27, 1958.

The following month, *Night Beat* went off the air, but Sanders went on to produce and write for other news shows. With the help of a full-time housekeeper, she continued to work after giving birth to a son, Jeff, in 1960.

In 1962, Sanders became assistant director of news at WNEW's sister radio station in New York. She edited the stories of reporters on the staff and learned how to go out and gather information for her own stories. That experience led to a job as a news correspondent at ABC-TV in New York City.

Soon after she began work at ABC, Sanders became the anchor for a five-minute daily news show, *News with a Woman's Touch.* The show came on in the afternoon when the main audience was women at home with their children. That was the only time slot open to female news anchors. People did not think that women were serious enough for the evening news.

Sanders broke that barrier one evening when the regular evening anchorman lost his voice. Sanders was asked to fill in. *The New York Times* gave her a good review, but it did not start a new trend in the evening news. "It was as if it had never happened," Sanders noted.[6] The next day, she went back to anchoring her daytime news show. Part of her job included going on location to gather news and do interviews for her show.

In 1966, Sanders was sent to Vietnam for three weeks to cover the war. A few other women had been in Vietnam as newspaper correspondents and photographers, but Sanders was the first in broadcasting. Many people thought it was too dangerous for a woman to cover the war. Sanders never came under enemy fire. However, she did get caught in a tear-gas attack when she was covering a Vietnamese student demonstration, which was broken up by South Vietnamese police.

The place where Sanders really made her mark in broadcasting was in writing and producing documentaries. She was known to tackle tough topics such as the right to die, child abuse, nuclear power, and the Equal Rights Amendment.

As Sanders advanced in her career, she worked to improve conditions for other women, both personally and professionally. An example was when she was selected to produce a documentary on women's health issues. Sanders insisted that no men would work on this show about women. "No male interviewer, no men on the crew," Sanders said.[7]

In 1976, Sanders was promoted, becoming the first female vice president at a major network. She used her position to change the hiring policies at the station by encouraging the hiring of more women and African Americans.

Sanders decided to leave ABC in 1978 when the head of the sports department was named news president. She did not agree with his ideas. Sanders said he wanted to make the news more entertaining; she wanted to do more serious news stories.

Sanders went to work in the news department at CBS. She did documentaries until the documentary division at the station was shut down. She then went on to produce and anchor news shows, such as *Sunday Morning* with Charles Kuralt.

Sanders suffered a personal loss in 1984, when her husband of twenty-five years died of a brain tumor. She was still adjusting to her loss when CBS began making huge cutbacks on the news staff in 1985. In the two years between 1985 and 1987, four hundred employees lost their jobs. In March 1987, another two hundred were expected to be laid off.

Sanders was offered a full-time radio position. She turned down the offer when she learned that she would be working night and weekend hours. Those hours were usually given to people just starting out in news. Instead, Sanders chose to make documentaries for a public television station in New York. From 1993 to 1995, Sanders was a professor at Columbia University's Graduate School of Journalism. She later began a teaching assignment at New York University's Department of Journalism.

Many people thought Sanders had been treated unfairly at CBS. Sanders said it was just business. Television news was changing. People had discovered that the news could make money. In order to bring in advertising dollars, news departments were making the news more entertaining. Employers were looking for a different type of personality. "They want perky — I'm straightforward," Sanders explained. "That's considered boring."[8]

During her thirty-three year career in news, Sanders won many awards for her work, including three Emmy awards. She wrote about her career and the careers of other newswomen in her book *Waiting for Prime Time: The Women of Television News*. The title refers to the fact that at the time the book was published in 1988, women still had not made permanent breakthroughs on prime-time news. "You can see women in the morning, they anchor over the

CBS-TV news correspondent Marlene Sanders gathers information for a news story on location in Detroit.

weekends, and they're on specials," Sanders noted.[9] Women had yet to be accepted as anchors on weeknight news shows.

Times have changed since then. Today, it is not unusual to see women anchoring the evening news. It was Marlene Sanders who took that first step.

Antonia C. Novello

Surgeon General of the United States

On March 9, 1990, Antonia C. Novello, M.D., became "a doctor for all Americans" when she was sworn in as surgeon general of the United States.[1] As surgeon general, she would keep Americans informed about health dangers and trends. She would also help form national policy on issues such as AIDS and smoking. Novello was the first woman and the first Hispanic American to hold that position.

Antonia Coello Novello, the daughter of Antonio and Ana Delia Coello, was born in Fajardo, Puerto Rico, on August 23, 1944. Her father died when she was eight, and her mother later remarried.

Tonita, as she was called by her family, was born with a colon disorder. The colon is part of the large

Antonia C. Novello

intestine. Tonita's colon problem caused her pain and made her stomach swell. She was told that she could have surgery to correct the problem when she turned eight. It did not happen. "I was one of those kids that got lost in the system of health, either because you're poor or either because your parents are not doctors, so you cannot ask the right questions," she explained.[2]

Because of her illness, Tonita spent at least two weeks in the hospital every summer getting treatment. But she spent no time feeling sorry for herself. "Life issues you a card, and you have to learn to play it," she later said.[3]

On the other hand, having a stomach that was flat one day and swollen the next was embarrassing for a teenage girl. Tonita relied on her sense of humor to help her cope. "I survived many times in my life by learning to laugh at myself—that's the best medicine," she said.[4]

She was active in school, where she played softball and sang in the school chorus. She was also an excellent student. Antonia's mother was a teacher who later became a school principal. She wanted Antonia and her brother, Tomas, to do well in school. "My mother felt that education was the key to a better life, and she pushed my brother and me to do our very best," Novello said.[5] Antonia graduated early and enrolled at the University of Puerto Rico when she was only sixteen.

Antonia was eighteen and in her third year of college, when she finally had surgery to correct her medical problem. There were complications with that first surgery, and she needed several more operations over the next three years. This illness fueled her desire to be a doctor. "I always felt I had to find a way for no one ever to go through this again," she said.[6]

Antonia earned her B.S. degree in biology in 1965 and enrolled in the university's medical program. She earned her M.D. degree from the University of Puerto Rico in 1970. The day after her graduation, she married Joseph Novello, a U.S. Navy flight surgeon who was stationed in Puerto Rico at the time.

Soon after their marriage, they moved to Ann Arbor, Michigan. They both continued their medical training there at the University of Michigan Medical Center. She specialized in pediatric medicine, and he studied psychiatry.

In 1971, Antonia Novello was named Intern of the Year by the University of Michigan Medical Center's pediatric department. It was the first time a woman received that award. Novello's internship was followed by a two-year residency program in Michigan. During that time, one of her favorite aunts died of kidney failure. Novello also suffered a serious kidney ailment. As a result, she decided to get specialized training as a pediatric kidney specialist. She began that training in Michigan and continued her studies at the Georgetown University Hospital in Washington, D.C.

Novello opened her own private pediatric practice in 1976, but she found it stressful dealing with her seriously ill patients and their parents. She gave up her practice after only two years. "When the pediatrician cries as much as the parents [of patients] do, then you know it's time to get out," she explained.[7]

There was also another reason for her career change. Many of Novello's young patients needed kidney transplants to survive. Novello was discouraged by how long they had to wait for an organ donation. Some of her patients did not get a transplant in time. Novello wanted to change that. She thought she could be more effective working in a government health care agency.

In 1978, she began work with the United States Public Health Service (PHS). The PHS is made up of several agencies, such as the Food and Drug Administration and the Centers for Disease Control and Prevention. The agencies of the PHS work with state and local agencies, conducting research, controlling disease, and keeping the public informed about health issues.

Novello also enrolled at Johns Hopkins University School of Public Health in Baltimore, Maryland. She earned her master's degree in public health from that university in 1982. She later completed a program for senior managers in government at Harvard University.

At the PHS, Novello concentrated on health issues related to women and children. During 1982 and

1983, she also worked with a U.S. Senate committee on two legislative projects. One was helping write the National Organ Transplant Act, which was passed in 1984. This law established a national network for acquiring human organs for transplants. Novello also helped draft the warning labels that are now found on cigarette packages.

In 1986, Novello took a position as professor of pediatrics at the Georgetown University School of Medicine in Washington, D.C. That same year, she was promoted to deputy director of the National Institute of Child Health and Human Development. One of her special concerns was pediatric AIDS, and she headed a task force to study the problem. It was her work with pediatric AIDS that caught the attention of President George Bush. He was looking for a candidate to replace the retiring surgeon general, Dr. C. Everett Koop. On March 9, 1990, Supreme Court justice Sandra Day O'Connor swore in Novello as the U.S. surgeon general.

As surgeon general, Novello was in charge of the more than six thousand members of the U.S. Public Health Service Commissioned Corps. The officers of this organization are medical professionals who hold ranks similar to those of the Navy. Members of the Commissioned Corps serve on American Indian reservations and in areas of the country where there is a shortage of doctors. They also do quarantine inspections at U.S. ports and are prepared to act in the event of a national medical emergency. As head of the Commissioned Corps, Novello had the rank of vice admiral. Her uniform was a navy blue suit accented with brass buttons and gold braid.

It was a rather formal uniform for Novello, whose office made a more casual impression. The waiting room to her office was lined with Cabbage Patch dolls, photos of children, and children's artwork. Although Novello has no children of her own, her love of children is obvious. As surgeon general, she often visited children in hospitals, hugging them and joking with them.

The position of surgeon general is a highly visible one. Novello often held press conferences to announce the findings of medical research projects. She also made fifteen to twenty appearances a week, speaking to Americans all across the country about health issues. She chose which appearances she would make from the more than one thousand invitations she received each month.

Novello focused on the special health issues of children, women, and minorities. She was concerned about the rising rate of smoking among young people and the number of underage drinkers. She criticized tobacco and alcohol companies that targeted these young people with their advertising. Novello also spoke out about the rising smoking rate among women. She cited the dangers of this trend, which included an increase in cases of lung cancer among women.

In 1992, Novello headed the National Hispanic/ Latino Health Initiative, a workshop held in

Novello visits children at a day-care center. As U.S. surgeon general, Novello targeted the special health issues of children, women, and minorities.

Washington, D.C. More than two hundred Hispanic leaders gathered to discuss the special health problems among Hispanic Americans. Their chief concerns were the number of Hispanic Americans who did not have health insurance and the health needs of migrant workers and undocumented aliens.

That year Bill Clinton was elected president of the United States. In keeping with tradition, Novello resigned so that Clinton could appoint his own surgeon general. Novello stepped down when Dr. Joycelyn Elders took over as surgeon general in June 1993.

Novello continued to keep people aware of health issues. She accepted a position as a special representative for UNICEF (United Nations International Children's Emergency Fund). In her new role, she traveled all over the world talking about health care for women and children. She held this job until 1996.

Since then, she has served as director of community health policy at the Johns Hopkins University School of Hygiene and Public Health and as a visiting professor at the university. She also worked toward a doctorate degree in public health at the university. In 1999, she was appointed New York State Health Commissioner. Novello hoped to make a difference for the children in her neighborhood in Puerto Rico, but she has helped millions more all around the world.

Chapter Notes

Chapter 1. Jane Addams
1. Gail Meyer Rolka, *100 Women Who Shaped World History* (San Francisco: Bluewood Books, 1994), p. 67.
2. Jane Addams, *Twenty Years at Hull-House* (New York: The Macmillan Co., 1942), p. 11.
3. Ibid., p. 7.
4. Ibid., p. 3.
5. Mark Kornblatt and Pamela Renner, "'Saint' Jane," *Scholastic Update*, February 23, 1990, pp. 10–11.
6. "Capital Is Saddened as Jane Addams Dies," *The New York Times*, May 22, 1935, p. 16.

Chapter 2. Madam C. J. Walker
1. A'Lelia P. Bundles, "Madam C. J. Walker: Cosmetics Tycoon," *Ms.*, July 1983, p. 91.
2. A'Lelia Bundles, "Madam C. J. Walker," *American History*, July/August 1996, p. 45.
3. Jill Nelson, "The Fortune That Madam Built," *Essence*, June 1983, p. 85.
4. Bundles, *American History*, p. 47.
5. Bundles, *Ms.*, p. 94.

Chapter 3. Harriet Quimby
1. Harriet Quimby, "How a Woman Learns to Fly," *Leslie's Weekly*, May 25, 1911, p. 602.
2. Harriet Quimby, "An American Girl's Daring Exploit," *Leslie's Weekly*, May 16, 1912, p. 579.
3. Henry M. Holden, *Her Mentor Was An Albatross* (Mt. Freedom, N.J.: Black Hawk Publishing Co.), 1993, p. 92.
4. Harriet Quimby, "The Dangers of Flying and How to Avoid Them," *Leslie's Weekly*, August 31, 1911, p. 249.

5. Harriet Quimby, "American Bird Women: Aviation as a Feminine Sport," *Good Housekeeping*, September 1912, p. 315.

Chapter 4. Jeannette Rankin

1. Norma Smith, "The Woman Who Said No to War: A Day in the Life of Jeannette Rankin," *Ms.*, March 1986, p. 88.

2. Hannah Josephson, *First Lady in Congress: Jeannette Rankin* (New York: Bobbs-Merrill Company, Inc., 1974), p. 19.

3. Smith, p. 88.

4. "Our Busy 'Congresswoman,'" *Literary Digest*, August 11, 1917, p. 43.

5. Robert D. McFadden, "Ex-Rep. Jeannette Rankin Dies; First Woman in Congress, 92," *The New York Times*, May 20, 1973, p. 65.

6. "Where Are They Now?" *Newsweek*, February 14, 1966, p. 12.

Chapter 5. Frances Perkins

1. "The Last Leaf," *Time*, May 21, 1965, p. 31.

2. George Martin, *Madam Secretary: Frances Perkins* (Boston: Houghton Mifflin Company, 1976), p. 42.

3. Deborah G. Felder, *The 100 Most Influential Women of All Time: A Ranking Past and Present* (New York: Carol Publishing Group, 1996), p. 42.

4. Ibid., p. 43.

5. Frances Perkins, "Eight Years as Madame Secretary," *Fortune*, September 1941, p. 77.

6. "Truce at a Crisis," *Time*, August 14, 1933, p. 12.

7. Perkins, p. 77.

8. "Truce at a Crisis," p. 13.

9. "Frances Perkins, the First Woman in Cabinet, Is Dead," *The New York Times*, May 15, 1965, p. 31.

Chapter 6. Pearl S. Buck

1. Dorothy Rompalske, "Pearl S. Buck," *Biography*, June 1997, p. 87.

2. Marjorie Dent Candee, ed., *Current Biography Yearbook, 1956* (New York: H.W. Wilson Company), p. 82.

3. "Earth to Earth," *Time*, March 19, 1973, p. 81.

4. Theodore F. Harris, *Pearl S. Buck: A Biography* (New York: John Day Company, 1969), p. 128.

5. Albin Krebs, "Pearl Buck Is Dead at 80; Won Nobel Prize in 1938," *The New York Times*, March 7, 1973, p. 40.

6. Harris, p. 216.

Chapter 7. Althea Gibson

1. "That Gibson Girl," *Time*, August 26, 1957, p. 45.

2. Althea Gibson, *I Always Wanted to Be Somebody* (New York: Harper & Brothers, 1958), p. 29.

3. Ibid., p. 66.

4. "Grand Slam: History of Blacks in Tennis," *Black Enterprise*, September 1994, p. 84.

5. Althea Gibson with Richard Curtis, *So Much to Live For* (New York: G. P. Putnam's Sons, 1968), p. 15.

Chapter 8. Sandra Day O'Connor

1. Garry Clifford and James R. Gaines, "Sandra Day O'Connor of Arizona: Portrait of the Justice as a Young Woman," *People*, October 12, 1981, p. 50.

2. Ed Magnuson, "The Brethren's First Sister: A Supreme Court Nominee—And a Triumph for Common Sense," *Time*, July 20, 1981, p. 12.

3. Ibid.

4. Pam Hait, "Sandra Day O'Connor: Warm, Witty, and Wise," *Ladies' Home Journal*, April 1982, p. 40.

5. Joan S. Marie, "Her Honor: The Rancher's Daughter," *The Saturday Evening Post*, September 1985, p. 42.

Chapter 9. Marlene Sanders

1. Edwin Miller, "Close-up," *Seventeen*, September 1973, p. 48.

2. Marlene Sanders and Marcia Rock, *Waiting for Prime Time: The Women of Television News* (Urbana: University of Illinois Press, 1988), p. 16.

3. Heather Twidale, "Personal Timeline," *Working Woman*, October 1985, p. 130.

4. Letty Cottin Pogrebin, "What Happened to Marlene Sanders?" *New Choices*, March 1989, p. 67.

5. Sanders and Rock, p. 21.

6. Jean Gaddy Wilson, "What It Takes to Be a Pro," *Working Woman*, October 1985, p. 130.

7. Beverly Schanzer, "Close-Up: Marlene Sanders," *Ms.*, February 1976, p. 19.

8. Pogrebin, p. 69.

9. Claudia Dreifus, "Marlene Sanders," *The Progressive*, October 1990, p. 38.

Chapter 10. Antonia C. Novello

1. Carol Krucoff, "Antonia Novello: A Dream Come True," *The Saturday Evening Post*, May/June 1991, p. 38.

2. Interview with Antonia Novello, M.D., June 18, 1994, Hall of Public Service, Academy of Achievement Web site, <http://www.achievement.org/autodoc/page/nov0bio-1>, January 26, 1999.

3. Charles E. Cohen and Teresa Riordan, "Butt Out, Guido Sarducci! Surgeon General Antonia Novello, Your Sister-in-Law, Wants Everyone to Quit Smoking," *People*, December 17, 1990, p. 110.

4. Krucoff, p. 40.

5. Diane Dismuke, "Meet: The Country's Doctor," *NEA Today*, February 1992, p. 9.

6. Judith Graham, ed., *Current Biography Yearbook, 1992* (New York: H. W. Wilson Company), p. 423.

7. Cohen and Riordan, p. 110.

Further Reading

Colman, Penny. *A Woman Unafraid: The Achievements of Frances Perkins.* New York: Atheneum, 1993.

Felder, Deborah G. *The 100 Most Influential Women of All Time: A Ranking Past and Present.* New York: Carol Publishing Group, 1996.

Fireside, Bryna J. *Is There a Woman in the House . . . or Senate?* Morton Grove, Ill.: Albert Whitman & Co., 1994, pp. 15–27.

Harris, Laurie Lanzen, ed. "Antonia Novello." *Biography Today.* Detroit: Omnigraphics, Inc., April 1992, pp. 62–66.

Harris, Laurie Lanzen, ed. "Sandra Day O'Connor." *Biography Today.* Detroit: Omnigraphics, Inc., July 1992, pp. 95–101.

Harvey, Bonnie C. *Jane Addams: Nobel Prize Winner and Founder of Hull House.* Springfield, N.J.: Enslow Publishers, Inc., 1999.

Herda, D. J. *Sandra Day O'Connor: Independent Thinker.* Springfield, N.J.: Enslow Publishers, Inc., 1995.

Holden, Henry M. *Her Mentor Was An Albatross: The Autobiography of Pioneer Pilot Harriet Quimby.* Mt. Freedom, N.J.: Black Hawk Publishing Co., 1993.

Hovde, Jane. *Jane Addams.* New York: Facts on File, 1989.

Morey, Janet Nomura, and Wendy Dunn. *Famous Hispanic Americans.* New York: Cobblehill Books, 1996, pp. 102–114.

Rolka, Gail Meyer. *100 Women Who Shaped World History.* San Francisco: Bluewood Books, 1994.

Rompalske, Dorothy. "Pearl S. Buck." *Biography*, June 1997, pp. 86–89.

Sanders, Marlene and Marcia Rock. *Waiting for Prime Time: The Women of Television News*. Urbana: University of Illinois Press, 1988.

Smith, Jessie Carney, ed. *Epic Lives: One Hundred Black Women Who Made a Difference*. Detroit: Visible Ink Press, 1993.

Wohl, Alexander. "First Lady of the Law: Sandra Day O'Connor." *Biography*, October, 1998, pp. 88–91.

Woolum, Janet. *Outstanding Women Athletes*. Phoenix, Ariz.: Oryx Press, 1992, pp. 103–106.

Internet Addresses

National Women's Hall of Fame
<http://www.greatwomen.org>

Jane Addams
<http://www.uic.edu/jaddams/hull/hull_house.html>
<http://www.nobel.se/peace/laureates/1931/addams-bio.html>

Pearl S. Buck
<http://www.english.upenn.edu/Projects/Buck>
<http://www.pearl-s-buck.org/psbi/PearlSBuck/about.asp>
<http://www.nobel.se/literature/laureates/1938/buck-bio.html>

Althea Gibson
<http://www.altheagibson.com>
<http://www.usta.com/bhm/gibson.html>

Antonia C. Novello
<http://www.achievement.org/autodoc/page/nov0bio-1>
<http://www.sg.gov/library/history/bionovello.htm>

Sandra Day O'Connor
<http://supct.law.cornell.edu/supct/justices/oconnor.bio.html>
<http://www.hws.edu/his/blackwell/bwaward/OConnor.html>

Frances Perkins
<http://www.wa.gov/esd/ui/ui101/frances.htm>
<http://www.dol.gov/dol/asp/public/programs/history/perkins.htm>

Harriet Quimby
<http://www.harrietquimby.org/index.html>

Jeannette Rankin
<http://www.wmst.unt.edu/jrf/story.htm>
<http://www.senate.gov/member/mt/baucus/general/bios/JeannetteRankin.htm>

Madam C. J. Walker
<http://www.madamcjwalker.com/index.html>

Index

Numbers in boldface type indicate photographs.